THE

Joy

OF

OWNING A

Soul

BY
STEVE EDSEY

Copyright © 2004
by Steve Edsey

1st Printing, September 2004

Printed in the U.S.A.

A.R.E. Press
215 67th Street
Virginia Beach, VA 23451-2061

Library of Congress Cataloging-in-Publication Data

Edsey, Steve, 1947-
  The joy of owning a soul / by Steve Edsey.
      p.   cm.
   ISBN 0-87604-496-8 (pbk.)
 1. Soul. 2. Life. I. Title.
   BD421.E35   2004
   204'.4—dc22

                              2004020404

CONTENTS

What are your favorite things?

What do you do
              to really enjoy this planet?

To get the most of it,
              how do you experience it?

Step back.
View yourself and your friends.

How do you
        enjoy the earth together?

You have a short time—
80 years, more or less.
What are your priorities on getting
the most of this experience?

Everyday you are faced with thousands of choices.
How do you choose?

And why?

> pleasure?
> need?
> personal reward?
> survival?
> duty?
> ego?

What are you building with this creation?
What makes your life your *own* life?
How are you known?

Part of the answer is
what you do—
your physical activities.

Name your favorite things.
Life is active.
Life is movement.

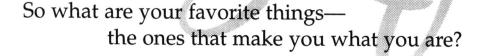

So what are your favorite things—
      the ones that make you what you are?

      What would you miss the most?
      What taken away from you really hurts?
      What is the most rewarding
                        and is now gone?

I share with you my list—
    being a daddy
    being a husband
    being a worker
    being a friend
    being active in sports
    being sociable.

Being denied these things is the end of life.
What is life with no activity?

What is your list?

What makes you you?

So, I am on earth...
I have experiences with stuff.
Stuff is things with shape,
                    weight
                        and size.

All stuff—all things—are important to me...
my tools, my car, my house,
my friends, my dogs, my
kids, my lawn, my golf
clubs, my clothes, my bed,
my books, my pen, my pho-
tos, my wife, my furniture,
my computer, my sports, my
old ties, my mother, my pic-
tures, my editor, my dictio-
nary, my credit card, etc.

All things have purpose in my life.
All things give my life meaning.

But without these things
is there no meaning?

At the end of my life, my things are left here.
I can't take them with me.

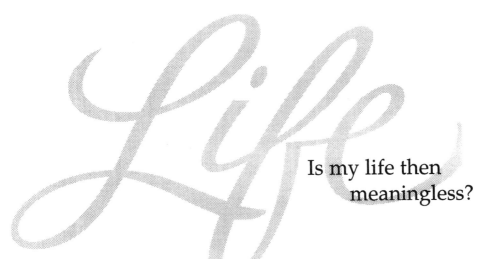

Is my life then
        meaningless?

My list of favorite things is based in the material—
only good for planet earth.

These things are non-transferable.
They stay.

I go.

A very tough law.

There must be meaning to things.

But what?

So,

what is the meaning in my list of favorite things?
what is the meaning if taken away?

A waste of time?
A good time for history?
A short joy?
A carnal pleasure?
A pleasure for the ages?
A bad example?
An image to be passed on?

Is there a soul to material things
                              that I do not see?

Is there a connection between
                              me and physical activity,
                              me and material,
                              me and things?

All material things are connected.
They are all matter—all common in make up.

What am I to realize here...

That material things are so simple,

so common?

There must be more to it.

There is a oneness to all things.

Science relates all material things in purpose.
Numerous books are written on laws of material.

It all means
a big
ZERO
at death.

Believe this.

All material things and all activities are

gifts of creative love from

a superior Father/Mother

sharing
their joy.

IT'S YOUR

Experience

This material experience
is just one experience of your eternal life.

Life is eternal.

There are many experiences of life.
Material earth is just one of them.

So the new question is...

From the material experience of earth
what do you take with you
to the next experience of life?

You definitely cannot take
your earthly body.

But what can you take?

The things you can take with you
must be of the greatest value,
because they are the only things
that can be transported during death.

What things are stronger than death?

We can easily eliminate material.

But is there a value to material?
          a virtue of material?
          a goodness,
            a godness,
               a soulness of material?

          Can spirituality
          of material things
          be transported to the future?

Only the feelings we place
in
our
souls,
our spiritual deposits,

can be transported to an eternal future.
In the depths of all events, activities and
thoughts are the potential for spiritual
deposits into the soul. These spiritual deposits
provide access to a spiritual future.

Spiritual deposits are a keycard to the future.

Look around you.

All material things,
    if activated properly,
        can be the channels for a spiritual future.

It is not the elimination of material but
        the spiritualization of material
        that leads to a spiritual life.

Material with a soul is life.
      You can breathe life into
                  this material experience.
         Earth lives because of the
              goodness God shares
with you.
      You raise a spiritless planet by
           taking material with no soul
           and giving it yours.

      You create life!

A channel of God's blessings flows
through you.
You have the capacity
to link with God's goodness
and influence earth.
The position of redeemer
is in your reach.
You can control your destiny.
You are given the opportunity
to share God's power.

The power of goodness—
what could possibly be
a better alternative?

In a state of humble acceptance you meet God in the temple of your soul. A feeling of total worthlessness befalls you with the realization that He lives within you. You are now anointed.

As He gave life to Adam, you will be His channel of life on earth.

As God breathed a soul into Adam,
He chooses you to breathe a soul into
your material experience.
You become

the savior of your experiences.

God emanates through your soul.
And you are humbled in His expectations.

What else on earth has this power?

Qualities of God are in you.

You are
the only channel of goodness on this planet.
You are
the only hope.
There is no other channel of love

but you.

You have the power to change material
into
a loving experience.
And this love
is your reward
to eternal life.

In love, through
material experience,
you create
the birth of
spiritual wealth.

Conception of spirit
becomes your reality.

Review your list of favorite things.
Look for its soul.
See the spiritual wealth in the list.
Look for the
love,
kindness,
understanding,
sharing and
goodness.
Develop the soul properties of your list.

Because,
my dear friend,
that spiritual wealth
is the only thing
you will take with you.

It is the treasure of your soul.
It is you.

On earth you are
the goodness you infuse into this material planet.

This belief is a large responsibility,
 but it is surpassed by the spiritual reward of
life eternal.

This life is one experience.

Your purpose is
to spiritualize the material.

One human being—
          you—with the powers of creation.

These powers are the powers of God.

With every event,
      every encounter,
      every material experience,
         you have the power
         to raise that experience to a higher level.
You have the power
         to raise that experience to the level of God.

         To live on earth
         and develop spiritual qualities
         can only be mastered by God.

You have been given this power.

The responsibilities of caring
            and maintaining this power
can only be entrusted to loving souls of the Lord.

If God believes in you,
            who are you to doubt Him?

Who are you
            that you
            should be empowered
            with qualities of God?

You can be that channel.
You can raise this planet to a level of God.

God believes you have that power.

You may feel unworthy of that destiny,
 but should be honored
with the potential of His calling.

Only
 because of His love of you and your purpose
is there life eternal—
a grand hope and joy
of
eternal growth and wealth.

Experience

Now with the view of being a channel of love,
review your list of favorite things.
Look into its soul, seeing the goodness of your list.
Spiritualize the list.
Induce values of a loving Father/Mother.

God has blessed each person
with part of His goodness.

Experience

What is your gift?
your talent?
your virtue?

Each soul has a beautiful gift—
an element of spiritual power.

It is hidden in your soul.
No person is alone.

What hidden treasure,
what secret blessing,
what value of goodness
is your personal gift to earth?

What spiritual talent
do you feel comfortable with?

This is a very personal decision.
No one masters all virtues.

But, for example, let us use *understanding*.

You have a friend.
  She listens.
  She questions.
  She never judges.
  She becomes one with your thoughts and
      completely understands your feelings.
You can tell her anything. And without judgement,
  she identifies and confirms your thoughts.
  She loves you for being you.

  There is a calm in your relationship—a trust.

Two souls
 form one
            through understanding.
And together
            through this understanding

        you have met God!

At that moment

you have been touched by God's love
through a friend.
The experience of
two souls living in the material planet
has raised the moment.
God's goodness
channeled through your friendship
has given life to the experience.

This is not
  a relationship based on
    material value that starts and stops on earth,

    but
  a relationship based on
    eternal principles that are everlasting—

a relationship that can be enjoyed FOREVER!

For this is now—
　　your treasure,
　　your purpose,
　　your future.

To take this time on earth
  and
  raise earth to a higher plane,

  give all experience a value in the spirit.

IT'S YOUR

Joy

IT'S YOUR

Soul

In this devotion three great things happen:

1. You put a soul into a dead planet—
   you add life, joy, love and caring.
2. You create a new event—
   an event conceived in the spirit of God.
3. You create your spiritual life
   in the next plane.

You are a spiritual being

havng a material experience.

You feel all that you truly learn.

To have knowledge is not to truly know.
To feel in your soul is to truly know.

Do you love?
How do you know?
Can you feel love in your soul?

Think of a person who loves you.

How do you know?

Prove it...with facts.

You can't.
You can list events.
But material proof cannot prove love.

You know you are loved

because

you *feel* loved.

You feel it in your soul.

All things of eternal value are things you feel
not through your senses alone
            but through your soul.

Material experiences spiritualized find
an eternal haven in you—
          a haven of joy
              you feel now and forever.

          God's love emanates from you.

          You are because you feel.

At the end of this journey
you look down on earth.

You see your neighbors, friends and family.
The good you have placed in these people's
lives reflects back to you as God's love.
You see your years on earth—
the love you shared as seeds of kindness
in the souls of your friends.
Because you have visited earth,
the planet glows with your love.

You have raised a planet,

Soul

and God loves you eternally.